Dennis the Menace

SHORT in the SADDLE

By HANK KETCHAM

FAWCETT GOLD MEDAL • NEW YORK

DENNIS THE MENACE—SHORT IN THE SADDLE

© 1976, 1977 Field Newspaper Syndicate

© 1979 Field Newspaper Syndicate

Published by Fawcett Gold Medal Books, a unit of CBS Publications, the Consumer Publishing Division of CBS Inc., by special arrangement with Field Newspaper Syndicate.

ISBN: 0-449-14287-6

Printed in the United States of America

First Fawcett Gold Medal printing: December 1979

10   9   8   7   6   5   4   3   2

"WHAT KINDA LANGUAGE IS *THAT*?"

"BASIC ITALIAN."

"I DIDN'T THINK THEY WAS THAT BIG!"

"I SURE LIKE GOIN' TO THE WALKERS'...THEIR
WHOLE HOUSE LOOKS LIKE MY ROOM."

"HE'S NOT JUST THE BEST OF HIS BREED...HE'S THE **ONLY**!"

"YOU LOOK REAL...AH...
NICE...DENNIS."

"GINA'S TOO POLITE
TO SAY 'STRANGE.'"

"HEY! THERE'S A PIECE OF CARROT IN MY SOUP!"

"WHADDAYAMEAN, NO EXTRA CHARGE?"

"IF THEY'RE HAVIN' WHAT I *THINK* THEY'RE HAVIN' FOR SUPPER ...LET'S GO TO A DRIVE-IN! OKAY, DAD?"

"WILL YOU PLEASE EXPLAIN TO HIM THAT, AT LEAST IN THIS HOUSE, FOOD IS TO BE TAKEN *INTERNALLY.*"

"...AND IF YOU'RE WORRIED ABOUT GETTIN' FAT, I'LL KEEP ALL THE FUDGE IN MY ROOM AND I WON'T LET YOU HAVE A *SINGLE PIECE!*"

"SOME GOOD-LOOKIN' KID OVER THERE WANTED TO
MEET YA...BUT I TALKED HIM OUT OF IT."

"SHE'S JUST CRAZY ABOUT BATHS. AFTER SHE WORKS ME OVER, SHE TAKES ONE HERSELF!"

"I WASN'T LISTENIN',
BUT I'LL FIND OUT."

"MARGARET WANTS TO KNOW
WHAT ALL THE YELLIN' IS ABOUT."

"WHEN I WAS A BOY, I DIDN'T HAVE A NICKNAME, DENNIS."

"NO KIDDIN'... *POTATO NOSE*?"

"THIS IS THE NICE LADY I WAS TELLIN' YOU ABOUT. IF SHE EVER WANTS TO USE OUR BATHROOM, BE SURE TO LET HER IN!"

"GEE, THAT HAPPENED BEFORE *LUNCH*, MR. WILSON! I DIDN'T THINK YOU WAS THE KIND THAT CARRIED A GRUDGE!"

"I THINK I FINALLY FIGGERED OUT WHAT'S WRONG WITH OL' MARGARET...SHE'S JUST *MARGARET*, THAT'S ALL!"

"HEY! DON'T I GET A DISCOUNT OR SOMETHIN' FOR TELLIN' THE TRUTH?"

"BUT YOU DON'T *SOUND* LIKE MY DAD.
YELL SOMETHING AT ME."

"MY DAD SAYS THE MOST EXPENSIVE THING ON FOUR WHEELS IS A SUPERMARKET CART."

"IF *DANIEL BOONE* LIVED HERE, SHE'D MAKE HIM USE THE BATHROOM!"

"YOU GOT LOTS OF TALENT, DENNIS...BUT DRAWIN' PICTURES ISN'T ONE OF 'EM."

"HOW 'BOUT YOU AN' ME JUST BEIN' GOOD FRIENDS FROM NOW ON ... INSTEAD OF *PALS*?"

"YES, I'M THE BABYSITTER...BUT...BUT I DIDN'T
REALIZE YOU WERE *THAT* MRS. MITCHELL!"

"I HAD TWO PACKAGES OF PIPE CLEANERS IN HERE..."

"NOW YOU HAVE ONE, LONG, SKINNY PIPE CLEANER."

"THIS IS THE BEST SMELLING STREET IN TOWN! A SHOE STORE AN' A CANDY STORE AN' A BAKERY ALL IN A ROW!"

"I'M NOT EITHER PLAYIN' WITH A GIRL! I'M PLAYIN' WITH **GINA!**"

"WOOPS."

"I CAN'T CALL ANYONE TO THE PHONE, MR. WILSON...THIS IS A RECORDING."

"DID YOU KNOW THERE'S A SECRET PASSAGE
FROM THE ATTIC TO THE BASEMENT?"

"YOU MEAN I WENT AN' WASHED MY HANDS
JUST FOR PLAIN OL' *TOMATO SOUP*?"

"*THAT'S* WHAT I'M GONNA
BE WHEN I GROW UP!"

"A BOY SCOUT!"

"As near as I can make out, some dumb girl *KISSED* him."

"I'M SURE GLAD I'VE STILL GOT *YOU*, MR. WILSON! I'M RUNNIN' *OUT* OF FRIENDLY NEIGHBORS!"

"HOW'S *THIS* FOR A COLLECTION? GOLD BRACELETS, DIAMOND RINGS, A MILLION DOLLAR WATCH AN'A *BILLION* PAPER CLIPS!"

"I HAD A GOOD FIGHT GOIN' FOR AWHILE...BUT THEY DECIDED TO KISS AND MAKE UP, AND NOW IT'S *LONESOME* AROUND HERE."

"SEE? HE'S NOT MAD AT YOU, MIZ GAGE...HE JUST DON'T LIKE BEIN' SAT ON."

"CAT, THAT IS MY BEST CHAIR!"

"HE SAYS, 'GOOD!'"

"IT'S GEORGE WILSON AND HE SAYS HE'S **FED UP!**"

"I'LL SAY...HAVE YA SEEN HIS *STUMMICK* LATELY?"

"WHEN MOM DRIVES, WE DON'T GET YELLED AT...
WE GET *WHISTLED* AT!"

"COWBOY TO RANGER...TWO SMOKEY BEARS HID OUT IN THE BUSHES HERE."

"IF WE GET LOST, WE CAN LIVE ON SNAILS AND BUGS!"

"IT MUSTA BEEN SOMETHIN' SHE *ATE*"

"WHAT IF I WON'T *EVER* SAY I'M SORRY? CAN I HAVE ANOTHER CHAIR FOR MY WIFE?"

"CAN I USE YOUR BATHROOM, MR. WILSON? IF I GO
HOME LIKE THIS, SHE'LL SCREECH ME OUTA A YEAR'S GROWTH."

"MAYBE HE BELONGS TO THAT LITTLE BOY."

" IS THAT YOUR KID OVER THERE?"

"THROUGH RAIN, SNOW AND SLEET...THAT KID'S GOT THE MAKINGS OF A GREAT *POSTMAN!*"

"THREE LITTLE PIECES OF MEAT AN' ELEVENTEEN CARROTS...YOU CALL *THAT* A BALANCED MEAL?"

"WANT ME TO TELL HIM OFF, DAD? HE WOULDN'T CLOBBER A LITTLE KID."

"DENNIS! HOW NICE YOU COULD COME AFTER ALL!"

"FORGIVE ME."

"SHOW MRS.WILSON YOUR NEW SUIT AND HURRY BACK."

"MR. WILSON SAYS I LOOK ALMOST *HUMAN*."

"I WORE IT THREE TIMES ALREADY... WHEN DOES IT STOP BEIN' MY NEW SUIT?"

"THERE'S A RIGHT AND A WRONG WAY OF HANDLIN' MR. WILSON."

"THAT'S THE **WRONG** WAY!"

"FALL IS KINDA LIKE A BUMPER, JOEY...IT KEEPS SUMMER FROM BANGIN' RIGHT SMACK INTO WINTER."

"DON'T BE SO POLITE...YOU'RE MAKIN'
THE REST OF US LOOK BAD."

"DAD SAYS TO GET THE **LEAD** OUT!"

"HONEST, HONEY, I MEANT **DENNIS**... NOT **YOU!**"

"I THINK MAYBE YOUR PHONE IS OFF THE HOOK, MR. WILSON...I KEEP GETTIN' A BUSY SIGNAL."

"DID YOU GIVE *HIM* A CHEAP CIGAR WHEN *I* WAS BORN?"

"LIKE I SAID... GINA DON'T LIKE NOBODY ELSE USIN' HER ACCENT."

"MMMMM...I BETCHA THE GUY WHO SAID ONE IN THE HAND IS WORTH TWO IN THE BUSH WAS TALKIN' ABOUT A TURKEY!"

"SOMETIMES I FEEL LIKE A MOTHERLESS CHILE...."

"I GUESS I'M JUST NOT AS THANKFUL ON SATURDAY AS I WAS ON THURSDAY."

"CLEANLINESS IS NEXT TO GODLINESS, YOUNG MAN."

"THEN WHY DOES HE MAKE MUD PUDDLES?"

"THEY SAY YOU HELP THEM THAT HELPS THEMSELVES...WELL...
THAT'S WHAT I WAS DOIN' WHEN I DROPPED THE COOKIE JAR."

"GEORGE WILSON RETURNING DENNIS' CALL...
HE SAYS BY GOLLY, IT *IS* RAINING."

"C'MON, LET'S GO, MOM! THERE'S NOTHIN' SADDER THAN
EMPTY REFRIGERATORS!"

"SHE'LL BE HERE IN A MINUTE. SHE'S TAKIN' HER CLOTHES OFF."

"HE COULDN'T WAIT... HE'S GONNA PHONE YOU!"

"I DON'T MIND THE *BATH* SO MUCH...EXCEPT AFTER
THAT EVERYTHING IS DOWNHILL TO BEDTIME."

"IF YOU WAS A CAT BEIN' CHASED BY A DOG, I BET YOU WOULDN'T HAVE TIME TO WATCH WHERE *YOU* WAS GOIN', EITHER!"

"YOU GONNA LET HER GET AWAY WITH *THAT*?"

"SAVE MY DESSERT!"

"MY EARS HEARD CHOMPIN' AND TOLD MY STOMACH, AND MY STOMACH SAID, 'WAKE UP'...THAT'S HOW I KNEW!"

"YOU CAN MAIL MY LETTER TO SANTA IF YOU WANT...BUT
I'D FEEL BETTER IF YOU SENT IT STRAIGHT TO GRANDPA."

"TELL HER TO GO 'WAY! I DON'T WANNA MEET *NOBODY* THAT USED TO CHANGE MY DIAPERS!"

"ALWAYS EAT THE FROSTING FIRST, JOEY...THEN, NO MATTER WHAT HAPPENS, YA ALREADY HAD THE BEST PART."

"SEE? EVERY TIME WE WALK THROUGH HERE, THEY ALL STOP TALKIN'...IT MUST BE SOMETHIN' JUICY!"

"WOW! THOSE PRICES ARE CRAZY! I GUESS I'LL JUST HAVE TO GIVE MY MOM THE QUARTER FOR CHRISTMAS."

"GOSH, THANKS A *MILLYUN*, GRAMPA!"

"NOW... WHERE CAN I GET A *SADDLE* ?"

"CAREFUL WITH OUR CREDIT CARD... MY DAD SAID IT SHOULDN'T GET *OVERHEATED*."

"I THINK HE'S FINALLY GONNA BRING ME A BROTHER... HE WANTS TO TALK TO YOU!"

"HE DIDN'T MEAN TO CALL YOU A DING-DONG... HE JUST DON'T KNOW VERY MANY WORDS YET."

"DON'T TRY TO REMEMBER EVERYTHING, JOEY...WHEN OL' SANTA ASKS WHAT YOU WANT, JUST *WING* IT!"

"MY MOM GOT LOST. CAN I USE YOUR LOUDSPEAKER?"

"DIDN'T MR. WILSON GET THE CHRISTMAS SPIRIT YET...
OR IS HE OVER IT ALREADY?"

"YEP, JOEY...WE'RE READY WHENEVER *HE* IS!"

"'CALM DOWN', SHE SAYS... LIKE IT WAS THE NIGHT BEFORE *FATHER'S DAY!*"

"HOPE YA HAD A MERRY CHRISTMAS, MR. WILSON...SAY, WILL YA LOOK AROUND AN' SEE IF SOMEONE LEFT A *PONY* OVER THERE BY MISTAKE?"

"HANG IN THERE!"

"BOY! NEEDLE CITY!"

"DON'T SAY NOTHIN' ABOUT BEIN' COLD AND WET...THAT'S THE *WORST* THING YOU CAN TELL A MOTHER."

"BOY! ONE OR TWO LITTLE SNEEZES AROUND HERE AN' ALL OF A SUDDEN YOU'RE FULLA HOT SOUP AND YOUR CLOTHES ARE GONE!"

"HEY, DAD... HOW COME **MY** LAP IS SITTIN' ON **YOUR** LAP?"

"I DON'T LIKE THE WAY THIS YEAR'S STARTIN' OUT."

"HOW 'BOUT ONE MORE FOR THE ROAD?"

"STAY *OUTA* THE ROAD," SHE SAYS."

"SINGIN'? WE THOUGHT YOU WAS YELLIN' FOR HELP!"

"DON'T WORRY, JOEY...SHE'LL GET OVER IT. MOMS HAVE A LOTTA TANTRUMS AT THIS AGE."

"THAT NEW KID THINKS DENNIS IS A SWELL NAME ...NOW!"

"YOU'RE PUSHING SOMEBODY ELSE'S BASKET, DENNIS!
OURS IS FULL OF VEGETABLES."

"HE CERTAINLY DOES FETCH SLIPPERS... I WONDER WHOSE *THESE* ARE?"

"DARLING... HOW CAN WE SAY GOOD-BYE?"

"LIKE THIS!"

"HOW CAN I GET IT WARM OUT HERE IF YOU KEEP CLOSIN' THE DOOR?"

"COOKIES AND CULTURE AT MARGARET'S HOUSE."

"WHAT **KINDA** COOKIES?"

"THE BROWN ONE'S A SHE-WA-WA...AND THE WHITE ONE'S A *HE-WA-WA.*"

"OKAY IF I EAT LUNCH AT THE WILSONS', MOM? HALF
THE PEOPLE OVER HERE WANT ME TO STAY!"

"I'M HOME EARLY 'CUZ MARGARET'S MOTHER DECIDED TO POSTPONE THE REST OF HER BIRTHDAY PARTY 'TIL NEXT YEAR."

"JUST TELL ME WHERE YOUR BATHROOM IS...
I'LL EXPLAIN WHEN I COME BACK!"

"I DON'T *WANT* MY PITCHER TOOK! YOU'LL CARRY IT AROUND
IN YOUR PURSE AN' TELL EVERBODY I'M YOUR *BOY FRIEND!*"

"MR. WILSON IS COMING OVER, DAD. YOU MIGHT BE THINKIN'
OF SOMETHING NICE TO SAY TO COOL HIM DOWN."

"HE'S TALKING IN HIS SLEEP."

"AND *ANOTHER* WAY YOU CAN DRIVE YOUR FOLKS BONKERS, IS TO..."

"HE **IS** ON A LEASH, BUT MY END OF IT CAME LOOSE."

"IF YOU EVER PLAY GOLF WITH *HIM*, DAD... YOU WON'T BE ABLE TO TALK TO THE BALL!"

"*BOY!* LITTLE MISS MUFFET NEVER LET OUT A SCREECH LIKE THAT ON *MY* RECORD PLAYER!"

"YOU SURE I'M ONLY FIVE-ANA-HALF? MR. WILSON SAYS HE'S AGED **TWENNY YEARS** SINCE I WAS BORN."

"HEY! I HEARD GINA GAVE YOU
SOMETHIN' FOR YOUR BIRTHDAY."

" BOY...WHAT A BEAUT!"

"HOW COME YOU SOCKED OL' MARGARET?"

"YOU KNOW MARGARET... TAKE YOUR PICK."

"YOU HAVE TO LIVE AND LET LIVE."

"IT'S AMAZIN' WHAT A SOCK IN THE EYE CAN DO FOR SOME PEOPLE."

"LEAST NOW WE KNOW DAD'S 'LECTRIC RAZOR DON'T WORK ON A COCONUT."

"BOY! IF FIRST GRADE IS ANY TOUGHER THAN KIDDIGARTER... I'M GONNA *FORGET* ABOUT GOIN' TO COLLEGE!"

"YOU'RE ALWAYS TELLIN' ME NOT TO DRAW ON THE WALLS...BUT YA NEVER SAID *NOTHIN'* ABOUT THE CEILING!"

"I'M NOT *S'PRISED* YOU'RE TIRED ... SITTIN' UP 'TIL NINE OR TEN O'CLOCK EVERY NIGHT."

"SIT DOWN, HONEY...HE'S JUST COUGHING TO COVER THE SOUND OF SOMETHING *ELSE* HE'S DOING."

"JOEY CHANGED HIS MIND, MOM!...HE *WANTS* SOME!"

"YOU *ALWAYS* GOT ROOM FOR DESSERT...
THAT'S WHAT *POCKETS* ARE FOR!"

"I'LL BET COWBOY BOB DOESN'T FUSS WHEN HE GETS A LITTLE SOAP IN HIS EYE."

"RIGHT... HE BELLERS!"

"IF YOU GET TIRED LOOKIN' AT **FOUR** WALLS ALL DAY,
YOU OUGHTA TRY JUST **TWO** WALLS SOMETIME!"

"OKAY...YOU CAN THROW THE NEXT ONE."

"A LITTLE *SLOBBER* NEVER HURT ANYBODY."

"YOU DON'T WANNA TAKE IT PERSONAL, JOEY...I BET MR. WILSON
HAS TOLD ME TO GO HOME A *MILLYUN* TIMES!"

"DID YA HEAR *THAT*, GINA? I WON THE CAKE-EATING CONTEST AND I DIDN'T EVEN KNOW THERE *WAS* ONE!"

"JUST SAY 'HELLO', HUH? IF YOU ASK HER 'WHAT'S NEW?',
WE'LL *NEVER* GET TO THE MOVIE!"

"MIGHT AS WELL MAKE IT A *DOUBLE* BATH....JOEY
WAS HIDIN' IN THE SAME GARBAGE CAN."

HERE COMES TROUBLE!!!
DENNIS THE MENACE!!!